MORN SQUEAKERS AND SCRAPERS

A MUSICIAN'S MEMOIR

[signature: Tony Spencer]

TONY SPENCER

Acknowledgements

In writing my memoir "Morning Squeakers and Scrapers," I would like to acknowledge the invaluable help of Sophie Wallace as my mentor and in editing this epistle.

I thank my parents for all their encouragement and sacrifices. And my teachers for their perseverance.

Lastly, I thank my wife, Mary, who took care of my home and my children, Chris and Helen, in all the months I spent abroad on band service.

CONTENTS
Page

Chapter 1

I cannot remember a time when I was not surrounded by music. My grandmother and grandfather on my mother's side played the piano and violin. Mum was a singer and introduced me to sing in various choral societies from an early age and my father always proudly boasted that he was a virtuoso in playing the gramophone.

In actual fact, Dad was more than that. He introduced me to the concert hall and after a hard day at work would rush home, have his tea, have a bath and then haul me off to a concert, or recital in London, or its suburbs. It was one of these performances that was to shape my career in the future. More about that later.

In family gatherings, such as birthdays, Christmas and other celebrations, a sing- song around the piano was almost certain to take place. With grandad playing his violin, accompanied by Granny, Mum and Dad singing, with auntie Doris joining in on her mandolin or banjo, her playing becoming more bizarre as she systematically emptied the sherry bottle.

My father's favourite party piece was to sing "Abdul the Bul Bul Ameer" whereas my mother's was "We'll gather lilacs in the spring again" or almost anything from Gilbert and Sullivan.

My earliest recollection of any sort of public performance was when my twin brother, Terry, and I appeared as a pair of candles in the pantomime, "Sleeping Beauty" presented by Chessington Methodist Sunday School. We were aged five and were obviously lead players!

At this time, Mother decided that Terry and I should have elocution lessons from a lady who turned up at the house on a weekly basis. These visits abruptly came to a halt when I told mum that I heard our eloquent teacher talking to someone else in the street, proclaiming "Bloody 'ell". That soon put paid to her attempting to get us to speak the "Queen's English". I might have told a little white lie, but that was the last we saw of her.

Mum and Dad met at a very early age through their love of ballroom dancing. They were in the first South of England Ballroom Dancing Team, formed by Frank and Peggy Spencer at the Royston Ballroom in Penge, South East London. Many a Saturday evening I would go with them and watch them dance, being fed with sweets from an enormous jar by Peggy. One evening I was suddenly lifted onto the stage and a pair of maracas were placed in to my hands. This was the first time I had ever played with a band. It couldn't have been better. I was in the presence of the great Joe Loss and his orchestra.

Whilst living in Chessington, my mother started me off on piano, but we moved to Hayes, in Kent where I started having lessons in the first year of Pickhurst Junior School at the age of eight.

The Head Teacher at Pickhurst was a man called Ken Pickering. He was a clever musician and every year, used to write the Christmas production and arranged all the songs for the school orchestra. He also put classical music on the record player for our entering the assembly hall and for our departure. Hiawatha's Wedding Feast was one of my favourites.

I took my grade one piano and violin exams in my fourth year of Junior school, my grandfather, by this time, having given me the half size instrument to play, that he had learnt on himself as a child.

In 1961 one of the most popular pieces ever written for the clarinet was recorded by Acker Bilk which became known worldwide. That is of course "Stranger on the Shore". It was 1962's biggest-selling single in the UK, spending 55 weeks in the charts. This piece made a big impression on me, but as I said earlier on, something happened in 1967 that inspired me further and that was a concert my dad took me to. It was a given in the Fairfield Halls, Croyden, by the Royal Philharmonic Orchestra. It was a Tchaikovsky night and I can still remember how much this music stirred my blood over fifty years ago. The ensemble, of course was magnificent, in particular, the soaring strings in "March Slave", but the best was yet to come. The last work in the concert was the 1812 Overture and the orchestra was augmented by the band of the Grenadier Guards. The musicians walked on to stage in their amazing scarlet and gold uniforms and I remember that the strings section of the orchestra was replaced in the band by a large clarinet section.

Well that was that, I was desperate to learn the clarinet. My parents were of limited means, but for Christmas they had managed to find me a second hand instrument as my Christmas present. It was a "Selmer Student Console" model and I am sure Mum and Dad had difficulty in affording its purchase. I can remember opening my present that Christmas morning, the smell of it, the beautifully polished wood and its shiny keys. I put the instrument together and my first sounds were just squeaks and squawks, but with the aid of my "Tune A Day" tutor book, I was able to make limited progress, so that on my final day at Pickhurst Junior, I managed to play my version of "Stranger on the Shore" as a farewell to my class teacher, Mrs Pococke, who immediately burst into tears. Weeping in delight I hope, rather than from distress!

Moving to Hawes Down Secondary School for Boys was a real shock to the system. The eleven plus examination was still in place and it was borderline as to whether I was sent to Grammar or to a Secondary Modern School. My parents decided that it would be better if I was at the top of the class in Secondary rather than to struggle at Grammar School.

The emphasis and the expectation at Hawes Down was that students be groomed more to going into an apprenticeship and learn a trade, rather than further education and academic study. The woodwork and metalwork shops were extremely popular and the favourite classes for many, but bullying was rife and that was just from the teaching staff. Of course it was a different era, but corporal punishment was dished out with frequency and relish at any misdemeanour committed. Public floggings in the playground seemed to be popular with some teachers where the punishment could be viewed by not just the whole school, but by any members of the public walking past the school railings at that time. If the unlucky recipient of these nasty assaults did not say "Thank you Sir", another wallop was received.

The one saving grace for me was the excellent music department led by a talented teacher and musician, Mr Norman Spurdens. He used to play the most incredibly virtuosic piano or harpsichord pieces to us during our daily assembly services and directed the most amazing boy's choir. More than this, he ran a department where those of us interested in music could retreat to at lunchtime away from the nasty bullying and humiliation culture that had been encouraged by many of the teaching staff.

I discovered that I had a pretty good boy soprano voice and for a little while I earned pocket money by being engaged as a soloist with many choral societies in the Bromley and Beckenham area

I continued my violin and piano studies with Muriel Schaefer, a fine violinist in her own right and Gwen Massey, who had been the accompanist of the great tenor, Heddell Nash. In school, I was equally fortunate in having clarinet lessons with two wonderful clarinettists, Bernard Parris and then, John Brightwell.

My instrumental teachers were keen that I took my associated Board Examinations throughout my time in school and encouraged me to enter competitive music festivals. I was very successful in these performances. I participated on the musical side of school shows and ensembles. I also joined West Wickham and Beckenham School's Orchestra as well as the Bromley Youth Wind Orchestra, of which I became principal clarinet. It's no wonder that nearly every school report at this time would finish with "If Spencer could put as much enthusiasm into his other studies as he does with his music, he could do well".

Again, at this time, aged twelve years old, something happened to steer my life for the future. I joined the Goldsmiths College Youth Orchestra. A fine group of students, conducted by Leonard Davies who was a violist in the Philharmonia. I would go to New Cross, in London, with my twin brother, Terry (who played the trumpet) every Saturday afternoon for rehearsal. I must confess to there being an ulterior motive on my part. In the clarinet section there was a young lady with a pretty smile, attractive long legs, that looked good in a mini skirt, and I took a shine to her. Little did I know at this time, but Mary Jarvis was to become my wife seven years later.

As I said earlier, I enjoyed taking my Associated Board performer's exams and aged fifteen took my grade eight on clarinet for which I received a distinction as well as taking grade seven at around the same time on piano and violin. In those days, a grade eight distinction could lead to a scholarship to one of the music conservatoires, but I would have had to have waited until I was eighteen to take advantage of this.

I don't think my parents were too happy about the events that were to unfold. I wrote to the Director of Music of the Band of the Grenadier Guards, Colonel Rodney Bashford, asking for an audition to join the Junior Musicians' Wing at the Guards depot, Pirbright, with a view to eventually joining the Band in Wellington Barracks, Birdcage Walk, London. Mum and Dad felt that I possibly wasn't good enough to get in, I should at least finish sixth form, and as far as Dad was concerned, I should go for a trade apprenticeship and enjoy music as a hobby. All of these points were valid, but I continued with my application all the same.

There were two vacancies for Grenadiers joining the Junior Musicians Wing at this time and five hundred applications. On audition, I was offered one of those places.

On 18th August 1971, aged fifteen and six months I enlisted into one of the most prestigious regiments in the British Army and started a new chapter in my life...

Chapter 2

THE JUNIOR MUSICIANS' WING OF THE HOUSE-HOLD BRIGADE

The Junior Musician's Wing was created as part of the Junior Guardsmen's company of the Guards Depot at Pirbright, near Woking in Surrey on 12th June 1962. It was similar to a sixth form college, training boys from the age of fifteen to seventeen and a half. If successful in their training, they would then join their respective regimental bands, or attend the Royal Military School of Music, Knellar Hall for a further year.

What a daunting prospect? I really wanted to be independent, so Dad dropped me off at Waterloo Station and I got on the train going to Brookwood in Surrey. There were many boys of my age on the train and judging by their accents, they had come from all over the country all travelling to join the Junior Guardsmen's or Junior Musician's wing of the Guards Depot. We were all intent on becoming members of the elite seven regiments of the Household Brigade. The Lifeguards, The Blues and Royals, being the Household Cavalry Regiments and the five Regiments of the Foot Guards; comprising of, the Grenadiers, the Coldstream, the Welsh, Irish and the Scots Guards.

Alighting at Brookwood Station, we were greeted by Sergeants from the depot who were immaculately dressed in their number two uniforms. We answered a roll call and were bundled, with our suitcases, into army trucks and taken the mile and a half to Pirbright Camp. At the barracks we were formed into squads and were marched, if you could call it that, to our accommodation. Here, we were introduced to Sgt. George Moulding, Scots Guards, who was going to take care our military needs. He informed us that we were an utter shambles. That we would be getting a proper haircut the next day. Also that we were to have a wet shave every day, whether we needed it or not. (a serious problem for the many of us teenagers with acne) After our little welcome pep talk, were then marched off to the cookhouse with arms swinging like windmills, before visiting the Quarter Master's store to collect our mattress and bedding.

The next few days were a whirlwind of visiting the stores to collect an assortment of uniforms and footwear, the promised shearing of the head and learning how to make a bedding pack. The aforementioned was inspected before breakfast every morning. My first attempts normally being thrown out of the window by the "Trained Soldier". Yes, that was a rank, and it was his duty to nursemaid us through all things military. He taught us how to "blanko" our webbed belts and polish our brasses and how to burn down our boots with a candle and dessert spoon and then layer them and spit and polish them with Kiwi shoe polish. Apparently nothing else would do.

We then had to prepare for frequent room inspections undertaken by Sgt Moulding, or officers of much higher rank.

They were expert in finding any speck of dust, checking that the floors had been polished to look like glass and certain to inspect that everything was present and correct in our lockers and in the prescribed place. Any misdemeanour here meant extra show parades, usually at the most inconvenient time as far as we all were concerned. I remember that some funding from my first pay parade (£3.00 per week) had to be used on the purchase of a new tooth- brush as the one I brought with me had to be used cleaning the plumbing in the washroom.

After a short time, getting us into some sort of "rookie" shape, we met our music teachers and instructors.

Our much loved Director of Music was Major W. Jackson MBE, affectionately known as "Jacko", but to his face "Sir". Prior to this appointment he had been the Director of The Band of the Lifeguards. A position he held until 1981. He was a brilliant clarinettist and a fine conductor.

Our Band Sergeant Major held the rank of Trumpet Major in the Lifeguards, a fine administrator and musician. Teaching clarinet and saxophone was Sgt Ronnie Pressland, Irish Guards. Sgts Dave Craft, Trombone Len Tyler, Tuba, John Dodd, French Horn. We also had some brilliant civilian professors on staff.

Our weekly training programme comprised of maths, English and military education. We also had lessons on our band and stringed instrument, or piano as well as rehearsals, drill instruction, P.T. and sport.

Our evenings were taken up with additional individual practice, kit cleaning and if all was well, we were allowed a brief visit to the NAAFI before "bed check" and lights out.

Our year was comprised of three terms and so there was always an end of term concert to prepare for. We were encouraged to take part in the Godalming and Woking music festivals and always did well on these occasions, bringing kudos to our establishment.

Awaiting inspection

Junior Musician Spencer on Clarinet

Our instructors were all members of Yately Symphony Orchestra that rehearsed every Wednesday evening. Along with a few other junior musicians I was allowed to join and getting out of barracks, mid-week was always looked forward to.

Our Saturdays were taken up with a morning on the parade square, where we as a band played slow and quick marches for the Junior Guardsmen to march around to. The afternoons were taken up with a sport of choice, mine being hockey, which I always enjoyed. I recall that on one of our Saturday morning parades it was very cold and frosty, and I was shivering uncontrollably. One of the officers on the square was Major Kim Ross, immaculately dressed, wearing his highly polished, brown riding boots, Sam Browne and leather gloves. He stood in front of me and said "Put your clarinet under your arm Spencer and place your hands together as if praying." With this he placed his gloved hands either side of mine, to warm them up. I've never forgotten that act of kindness to this day. Major Ross went on to become Colonel of the Scots Guards and then Brigadier, Governor of the Royal Hospital, Chelsea.

On another occasion the Sgt Major saw flowers had been planted outside the band accommodation and started yelling at everyone, shouting "Who has put these flowers here?" It just happened that Major Ross was passing by. "I did Sgt Major." The response was "Well ain't they f****ng pretty Sir" much to the amusement of the band.

Sunday mornings were generally taken up with church parade, often I was the organist. I was paid the princely sum of one pound per service and soon realised that I could fit in Church of Scotland, of England and also Mass at the Roman Catholic Church. Doing this doubled my weekly salary. On those wages I could afford to invite my girlfriend Mary down to Guildford for Sunday lunch at the Berni Inn. See-ing Mary and having a steak dinner with a glass of Cote de Rhone was always a treat I looked forward to.

Major (Jacko) Jackson gave us all many opportunities. 1972, the band travelled on a courtesy visit to Malmö in Sweden on HMS Ulster. Conditions were very cramped on board and so we had to have our meals on deck. This was fine, but two musicians each day were detailed to do the washing up. Disaster! On the first day out from Portsmouth, our washer uppers threw all our cutlery overboard with the washing up water. What a display! The ship's propellers volleyed up the knives, forks and spoons back into the air with the sound of a manic percussion section and the impressive sight of a metallic Roman candle. Then there was a sudden silence from all around with the realisation that we would be eating with our fingers until we could purchase replacement cutlery after docking in Sweden.

It was a great trip, watching naval manoeuvres, performing for the ship's crew and at various locations in and around Malmö. On the way home we had to disembark at Harwich. A minesweeper came out to pick us up, which was rather precarious as we had to time our jump from one ship to another in a force 6 gale. Fortunately everyone landed on to the deck of the smaller ship safely except for Jacko's peaked cap, that went flying off into the distance.

Pirbright also gave me the opportunity to be a movie star. In 1973, a couple of us took a trip to Shepperton Studios where the film "Bequest to a Nation" was being shot. Originally a novel by Terence Rattigan, about Lord Nelson and Lady Hamilton, starring Peter Finch and Glenda Jackson. Off-screen we had to be recorded playing recorders, but for the film we were dressed up as drummer boys on board HMS Victory, playing fifes and drums amid the chaos of the Battle of Trafalgar. I think the view of us in the film is for less than thirty seconds, for which we received the incredible fee of twenty-seven pounds each. I had never been so well off!

The Summer term, 1973 was my last at the Junior Musicians Wing, Pirbright. I had won a Worshipful Company of Musicians prize, awarded by Imogen Holst for outstanding musicianship. I was also awarded my A1 trade qualification by Colonel Duncan Beat, Director of Music, Scots Guards Band. This was unusual for a musician still on "boy service". Army musicians in those days were graded into A3, A2, and A1 being the highest trade pay award.

My final pass out parade and farewell to Pirbright came at the end of June. I was eager to move on and had my cases packed before the parade started. Mum and Dad attended, as did Mary. A farewell buffet was organised for us all and then it was "By the left. Quick March!" on to the next Chapter in my musical adventure.

Chapter 3
The Royal Military School of Music, Kneller Hall

Kneller Hall was originally called Whitton Hall, named after the village it was built next to. In 1709, it was purchased by Sir Godfrey Kneller and renamed Kneller Hall.

On 3rd March 1857, it was purchased by the War Office as a training establishment for army musicians. Many famous instrumentalists, Bandmasters and future Directors of Music passed through its doors. Kneller Hall closed its doors as a military establishment in 2021.

In September 1973 I walked through the gates of the Royal Military School of Music, passed the guard room and was immediately in awe of the magnificent building that was Kneller Hall.

One of the permanent staff welcomed us and gave us a tour of the site. There were two accommodation blocks, with the cookhouse between the two. On the other side of the main building were tennis courts. Hours of fun were had with ball and racket, albeit I played very badly. The concert hall was out of bounds as the roof had collapsed and instead a sound dome which was like a grounded, inflatable balloon had been erected. It was a great performance area, except that one could hear the sound of the huge fans that kept it inflated. Then there were the sports fields adjacent to Twickenham Stadium rugby ground.

Grand open air concert

Finally we passed the hallowed ground, fondly known as the rock, the area where, from June, through to September we performed the famous Summer season concerts.

As pupils of KH we were divided into four company bands. A, B, C, and D, with a third year Student Bandmaster as Company Commander. I was in D company and ours was the well liked and affable Std BM John Simmonds, a flautist and a fine conductor. My barrack room accommodated some overseas pupils including two from the Hong Kong police force band, two from Brunei and one man from the Bermudian defence force band who was over six foot tall, but played the piccolo, smallest of all the military band instruments. Despite being from such diverse backgrounds, we all got on really well together.

Our days were filled with tuition on our first and secondary instruments by civilian professors, many of whom came from the London Orchestras and also taught in the London Conservatoires. We also had company and whole school band rehearsals, lessons in harmony, orchestration and aural training. There was a daily morning service in the chapel, where you either sight-sung in the choir, or sight-read and transposed out of the hymn book if you were playing in the accompanying band. The chapel was where Sir Arthur Sullivan had played the organ, as his father, Thomas Sullivan, was an instrumental professor from around 1816 after being an instrumentalist in the band of the Royal Academy, Sandhurst.

Monday evenings were taken up rehearsing with the number 1 playing out band, consisting of student bandmasters and pupils if proficient enough. This ensemble used to "fly the flag" for military music and perform at engagements throughout the south of England. I was very fortunate to be a soloist at many of these concerts.

Wednesday afternoons were timetabled for sport and you had a choice of what you wished to do. My choice, along with many others was to go to the swimming pool in Twickenham, purchase a ticket as proof of attendance and then take time off to spend an afternoon of leisure.

All pupils were allocated non musical weekly tasks such as sweeping the parade ground, litter picking and leaf collecting. In the Summer season there were deck chairs to be put out and put away for our audiences. Programme sellers were also needed. Programmes were sold at the princely sum of 5p.

They say that in the army never volunteer for anything, but the school required someone to man the telephone exchange in the mornings before the civilian telephonist arrived to take over at 9 a.m. I took up the challenge and it soon became evident that it was to my advantage. I used to take my clarinet into the exchange for 7.a.m, work the switchboard as required and ring my Mary every day to get her up for school. Volunteering for this job made me exempt from these other tasks.

Occasionally I was asked to work the telephone exchange at weekends. This was because KH was used as a communications post for military exercises taking place throughout the UK.

I was fortunate to have served under two eminent Directors of Music whilst at KH. Firstly Lieut. Col. Rodney Bashford, who retired halfway through the year and then Lieut. Col.Trevor Sharpe who was appointed to the post. Two very colourful characters and famous throughout the military band world. The Summer concert season ran from the beginning of June until the second week in September.

The rehearsals for these concerts took place most days during the Summer and I always found them to be great fun. It was an opportunity to take the student bandmasters through their paces, observed by the Director of Music. For each concert one student was required to compose and conduct his own composition. It was not unknown, if Col. Rodney was displeased with a poor student's efforts, for him to address the whole band thus: "Gentlemen. Pick up the manuscript placed in front of you, the right hand side with your right hand thumb and forefinger and the left hand side with your corresponding thumb and forefinger and pull in opposite directions." The poor student seeing hours of work being ripped up in front of his very own eyes. Rodney would then order the student to rewrite his grand opus ready for the final rehearsal and concert performance.

I learnt many things from observing their conducting techniques, some of which were rather bizarre. For example, Rodney Bashford had a peculiar way of starting off the second movement of Gustav Holst's Suite in F for Military band, named "The Song of the Blacksmith". The first bar is in 4/4, though in mixed metre throughout. It also starts on the second quaver leaving the first silent. Rodney used to literally kick it off with the stamp of his foot. It seemed to work really well. Trevor Sharpe's conducting was very flowery and it was often said that it was likened to a sword swinging display.

Apart from both of these Directors of Music being good conductors, they also produced many fine compositions and arrangements that were and still are a great addition to the wind band repertoire.

On the weekly timetable at KH were the conducting classes for the student bandmasters taken by professor Maurice Miles. We, as pupils provided the bands for the students to conduct. A very amusing experience for us, but quite terrifying for many a student on the rostrum.

Maurice was the first conductor, at that time, of the recently formed Ulster Orchestra and regularly conducted the BBC Welsh and Scottish Symphony Orchestras. In addition, he was conducting professor at the Royal Academy of Music in London. A man with a very red face and long white swept back hair, and with a temperament not to be trifled with, who left many a conducting student trembling after a session with him.

Maurice was however, a very kindly man and gave me the opportunity to perform both of Weber's Clarinet Concertos with the West London based Ealing Symphony Orchestra and to perform with many other ensembles.

My clarinet professor at Kneller Hall was the eminent clarinettist Paul Harvey. Born in Sheffield in 1935, he studied clarinet with Frederick Thurston and Ralph Clarke. He became a member of the Band of the Irish Guards, the Scottish National orchestra and the Bournemouth Symphony Orchestra.

I spent many hours listening to his words of wisdom and gleaning as much knowledge as I could about the technicalities of playing the clarinet, about the art of performance itself and many, many anecdotes of his experiences in the profession. Again he was a man who gave me many opportunities for solo performance, both at Kneller Hall and also in the outside world.

In March 1974, Paul directed a concert by the Kneller Hall Clarinet Choir entitled "A Salute to Gordon Jacob". Gordon Percival Septimus Jacob CBE was an English composer and teacher. He was a professor at the Royal College of Music in London from 1924 until his retirement in 1966. The concert was to celebrate Dr. Jacob's eightieth birthday. He was in attendance and I had the honour on this occasion to perform his Concertino for Clarinet accompanied by the clarinet choir. I still have the music that I played from, autographed by the great man himself, *"Gordon Jacob, with great appreciation."*

Tony Spencer, performing the Tartini/Jacob Clarinet Concertino.

My year at the Royal Military School of Music, Kneller Hall was coming to a close, but there was one final accolade to reach out for. The Cousins Memorial competition for the best instrumentalist of the year.

In 1863 Charles Cousins was appointed Bandmaster of the 2nd Dragoons and in 1874 became the Director of Music at Kneller Hall, a post he held until he suddenly died in 1890. The Cousins emorial prize, in his honour, was presented once a year to the best instrumentalist. In 1974 Paul Harvey wrote a work for unaccompanied clarinet that he dedicated to me, titled "Improvisation on a Martial Inversion". I am happy to say that I performed this in the competition and won first prize. I was awarded the parchment and silver medal by Mrs. Ursula Vaughan Williams at the end of year awards ceremony.

My final concert at Kneller Hall was on Wednesday 11th September 1974.

This concluded three years of study as a military musician. The Army had given me some incredible experiences and opportunities in this time. I made friends that I'm still in contact with to this very day.

The next chapter in my life was to earn my living as a professional army musician in the Band of H.M. Grenadier Guards.

CONSILIO ET MEMORIAL

Royal Military School of Music.

KNELLER HALL.

This Certificate is awarded to

A. Spencer

for exceptional Proficiency on the

Clarinet

DIRECTOR OF MVSIC.

COMMANDANT.

Dated this 19ᵗ day of SEPTEMBER 1974

Chapter 4

I joined the Band of the Grenadier Guards, based at that time in Chelsea Barracks in the middle of September 1974. The band that I had the privilege of being with for the next fourteen years.

To write about all my experiences would certainly take up at least a couple of volumes. I left the band over thirty-five years ago and so some memories will have faded into the mists of time, but I was to embark on the most exciting adventure anyone could have wished for, as a day job.

I arrived on my first morning punctually at the band office to find everyone busy polishing brasses, whitening belts, card cases and bayonet frogs, spit and polishing boots and grooming Bearskins (or Bearskin caps as they should be really known).

We had to report to Jim Norris, the Band Sergeant Major, who was in the band library and like everyone else was busily preparing to get on parade. The band was to lead the new guard, from Chelsea, up Buckingham Palace road, past Victoria station and into the forecourt of Buckingham Palace for the ceremony of changing the guard. Major Peter Parkes, the Director of Music walked into the library. "Good morning gents, we've been expecting you". I looked around to see who he was talking to, before I realised that he was addressing us. I had already served in the army for three years and had been called many things, but not a gent! The major continued "We are just going out for guard mount, but we'll introduce ourselves properly when we get back later on."

The Regimental Band, November 1974

The band formed up and on the command of the Drum Major marched onto parade. We, accompanied by the band librarian, stood on the edge of the parade square to watch the proceedings. The band in position, an order was screamed out, "New Guard. Get On Parade". The guardsmen then marched onto the square and formed up ready for inspection. The officers casually patrolled up and down in front of the troops, until the adjutant arrived. At one point in the proceedings, there was a bugle call and the order was given "Present arms". It was helpful having an old soldier with us, who hastily told us to stand to attention. We were dressed in our civilian suit, collar and tie, but etiquette still had to be observed. The colour was escorted onto the square in preparation to lead the men to their duties. Again, as the new guard, with the band playing the march, Colonel Bogey, marched off, we rigidly stood to attention. As the sounds of the band drifted away it was time for a cup of coffee in the band library and await their return.

It was not long before we heard the band on its way back in to barracks, or rather the first thing we heard was the pulsating beat of the bass drum. As the old guard, led by the band came in to view the strains of "The Grenadier's Return" were heard. Time to yet again stand to attention as the colour was escorted back to its home in the officer's mess. The band was then dismissed from parade.

There were no other duties for the band that day and so the band members got out of uniform and went their separate ways. I later learnt that many of the musicians had part time jobs for when they were not required for band duties. Many were peripatetic teachers visiting schools in the locality, but one I knew of had a prosperous window cleaning business and another worked in Billingsgate fish market.

In a matter of minutes, Jim Norris, Band Sergeant Major, took myself, along with Simon Locke and Al King into the Director of Music's office to be officially welcomed by Major Peter Parkes. "Gentlemen, you all have had glowing reports from Kneller Hall. Well done." He continued, "You are now joining one of the finest military bands in the British Army and we have a reputation to maintain. Wel-

29

come and if you have any problems speak to the Band Sgt. Major and my door is always open."

Leaving the D of M's office Jim informed us that there was very little accommodation and we would have to sleep in a classroom upstairs. Report to the Quartermaster's Stores to collect your bedding. Go and settle in and I shall see you in the morning ready for band practice. Make sure that you are sat down in the chapel ready to start the rehearsal by 9.50 dressed in your suit collar and tie.

I must mention at this point that members of the band at this time were not required to wear uniform unless on parade or for a concert performance. This tradition dated back to the time when the regiment employed civilian musicians. We were expected to wear a smart suit or blazer and tie. Any musician not coming up to standard would be required to revert to army uniform.

The next couple of days were taken up by learning our trade, such as visiting the forecourt of Buckingham Palace to observe what was required of the band during the ceremony known as "Changing the Guard". We had sets of march cards issued. Music printed small enough to be carried by lyre shaped clips attached to our instruments. We had to have Bearskins issued and fitted and had to go and get measured for our ceremonial uniforms.

Visiting Kashket Tailors in Hoxton Square, just off Old Street was a real eye-opener in more ways than one. They had the contract to make all the ceremonial uniforms for the Guards, the Yeoman Warders and the Queen's Bodyguard. Kashkets is a Jewish family from Chigwell. They can trace their history back to being hatters at The Court of the Russian Tsar in the early 1900s. We had to meet at the tailor's shop for 11.00 am and were met by two elderly men who were to take all the measurements required and chalk up the beautiful scarlet cloth. We were then informed that we should go for lunch whilst the cutters got to work, ready for an initial fitting in the afternoon. Little did we know what they had in store for our lunchtime venue. The place of choice, that was their choice, was a pub around the corner in Old Street called Horns. We walked in and it was packed out with office workers from the locality. We soon realised the popularity for all assembled, including our hospitable tailors. It was a strippers pub and as our eyes became acquainted to seeing through the fog of cigar and cigarette smoke, we could see naked women wandering around, collecting money in pint beer mugs.

I soon realised it was not a collection for Dr. Barnados. I was also soon to realise that, in years to come, when being measured up for a new uniform, this was where our sociable tailors expected to be taken for lunch.

I must at this point make mention of my first boss, or as we called him, "The Governor", Major Peter Parkes. He was an amazing conductor, a perfectionist and he demanded perfection from all of those under his baton. He was certainly a workaholic and apart from being our director he was the conductor of The Black Dyke Mills Band as well as many other brass bands across the UK.

In 1974, we went to Buckingham Palace to record the National Anthem for the Queen's Christmas Day address. She must have been listening in, as we received the message that our interpretation was far too slow and pompous and so we re- recorded it. The band frequently performed at Buckingham Palace garden parties and on one occasion, yet again, Her Majesty informed us that we were playing the anthem at the wrong tempo and on this occasion actually "La-la-ed" her way through the first stanza to get her point across.

In no time at all I had got into the routine of Guard mounting ceremonies at Bucking- ham Palace and at Windsor Castle, known as public duties. We also spent a lot of time, particularly at weekends, travelling around the country giving concert performances. I always enjoyed getting on the coach, travelling up the motorway to towns and cities that I had never visited before; Coventry, Bradford, Cardiff, Manchester and many, many more. The excitement of setting up and rehearsing our concert in a new venue, be it a Victorian town hall, or modern theatre. Apart from the playing, I loved meeting and chatting with our concert goers during the interval. It seemed somehow to give a better insight into the places we were visiting. On the downside in those early days, most cafes and restaurants were closed on a Sunday. It was best to pack a sandwich.

During the week, we spent many evenings playing in some of the top London hotels, mainly to tourists, playing in cabaret, or as they were officially known, Ceremonial Marching Displays (CMDs).

Another part of our time was taken up in recording studios producing LPs and with the BBC doing recorded and live performances. BBC recordings usually took place at the Maida Vale Studios and included shows such as "Bandstand", "Marching and Walzting" and "Listen to the Band". We also joined up with the BBC Concert Orchestra on occasions for "Friday Night is Music Night", live from Golders Green Hippodrome.

Early on in my career, it was decided at Horse Guards that all musicians of the Household Division should have a secondary role as Medical Assistants. For many bands within the British Army this was nothing unusual and musicians had been employed, in time of war as stretcher bearers, but to us, it was a little bit of a shock. Apart from the medic training, learning to fire a submachine gun was part of our new job description. Playing a clarinet seemed easier to me than hitting a target on the range and it was nothing for me and some of my colleagues to be seen running towards the said target so that we could pierce it a couple of times with a sharp pencil, before the instructor got to it. I must say that the basic medical training that we received came in very useful. On one occasion, singing in a choir rehearsal, an elderly man in the pew in front of me collapsed and appeared to stop breathing and I was able to confidently give him CPR until the ambulance arrived.

In 1978/79, there were many strikes in what was called The Winter of Discontent. The London Ambulance service went on strike a couple of times and our newly acquired skills were put to good use and we manned the ambulances for a short period. At this time I was based at Shooter's Hill Police Station and my patch was the Old Kent Road up to the Elephant and Castle. Most of my duties were routine, getting elderly folk to and from hospital appointments, or getting pregnant women, who were in labour to the maternity ward. My driver and I did however, blot our copy book early one evening during the rush hour. We happened to be right at the top end of the Old Kent Road towards the end of our shift and we wanted to get back to the police station for our supper. I told my driver to switch on the flashing light and the siren and weave in and out of the rush hour traffic. To my horror and just a few seconds too late I saw an elderly lady with a Yorkshire terrier on its lead that was having a pee in the kerbside gutter, suddenly the lead was dogless. We were, of course given a severe reprimand, although we denied all knowledge of the event.

Chapter 5

"Come into my office and close the door Tony", the BSM Jim Norris said. Was I in trouble? What had I done? "It is my sad duty to inform you that your parents have just rung to say that your Grandfather passed away this morning." It was January 29th 1976, my case was packed and I was ready to embark on my first major tour with the band. Jim continued. " You may have compassionate leave to be with your parents and attend his funeral, but your parents felt it would have been his wish that you go with the band to Hong Kong."

I rang Mum and Dad back, they repeated what Jim had told me and they wished me Bon Voyage. With a heavy heart, I sadly got onto the coach that was to take us to RAF Brize Norton. Staying at the base overnight, we flew out on an RAF VC 10 the next morning. Just the flight was an amazing experience. As if perfectly timed, the pyramids in Egypt came into view as the sun arose on the horizon. Our first stop was in Bahrain and then Colombo, Sri Lanka. Landing there was interesting, to say the least, as we descended through the storm clouds of a monsoon. After landing, the cabin doors were opened and we were immediately soaked in sweat; the humidity and the temperature was so high even though it was the middle of the night. It didn't help as we always travelled in suit, collar and tie.

In those days, Kai Tak was the international airport in Hong Kong and the runway went far out into the sea. The landing to me was spectacular as it seemed that we would land in the sea, but at the last moment we touched down on terra firma. Little did I know that, taking off, homeward-bound was even more thrilling as our aircraft seem to weave through the tower blocks of Kowloon.

Our destination, Stanley Fort was on the south side of Hong Kong Island and to get there we had to travel over the Peak, the highest point on the Island, which gave us spectacular panoramic views of Kowloon and the Wanchai.

We had been travelling for over twenty-four hours, but after getting settled into our barrack accommodation, sorting out our bedding and unpacking our uniforms we were unde-terred from catching a bus, travelling back over the Peak to seek out the nightlife of the Wanchai. I was dazzled by the sights and sounds and the hustle and bustle of oriental city life. Also, the smells of the cooking from street vendors, from burgers and hot dogs to the more exotic like Jaa jyu cheung (fried pork intestine) and Gaa lei yu dan (curry fish ball). We, of course, had to visit a couple of bars. Cold beers served by Chinese hostesses, mostly topless and trying to entice you in to buying them a very expensive 'Hostess cocktail' and leading you to a curtained alcove with the promise of more pleasures to come. Fortunately, we had all been given a briefing at the barracks before being let loose and declined all such offers.

We were visiting Hong Kong by invitation of the second battalion Grenadier Guards who were serving there and stationed at Stanley Fort. They were excellent hosts and went out of their way to act as our tour guides. We were taken to a border observation post in the new territories, overlooking the Sham Chung river, where many poor souls were shot at by the communist Chinese whist trying to escape across the border. Sadly, if they survived crossing the river and were caught by the British Border Guards, they had to be handed back into the custody of the Chinese to await an unknown fate. In the New Territories there were many walled towns and villages, usually with just one entrance and very narrow streets. We were taken to one such village named Kam Tim. We were warned not to wander around by ourselves, but in small groups. It was said that many of these enclaves were controlled by the triads. My memory of the visit was one of silence except for the tapping of Mahjong tiles and the pungent smell of opium, as it was the habit of many of the inhabitants to "Chase the Dragon".

Our visit was not entirely a holiday. We played in small ensembles in the Sergeant's and Officer's messes and in the canteen for the other ranks. Also for a families barbecue, Church services and a beating retreat, joined by the battalion's corps of drums, sounding the last post on the immaculate lawn in front of the officer's mess as the Union flag was lowered and the sun set over the China sea. Other duties undertaken whilst in Hong Kong were taking part in the Arts Festival and a tour of schools on the Island and New

Territories giving demonstration concerts to their students, both primary and secondary.

The band performing in Stanley village.

Down the hill from the barracks was Stanley Village, now a large, built up holiday resort. In 1976 it was a small traditional fishing village, with fascinating small shops. Some, not for the faint-hearted, selling such delicacies as snake bile wine and demijohns packed full of fermenting starlings. The butcher had dogs hanging up on meat hooks for sale and other things in trays, unidentifiable by me. In the market there was an amazing array of fish and crustaceans. I observed the more well off taking the main part of a fish, whilst the head and the tails were tossed into a bucket to sell to the poor. There were live chickens and ducks for sale that were hastily despatched before the customer. The entrails put into a trough for the live poultry to feed on. Children were sitting on the kerb side chewing on raw chicken feet for nutrition. In one of the grocer's shops, you could walk through the back where an elderly woman cooked Young Chow, a delicious fried rice dish which contained various meats (no I didn't ask) prawns, spring onions and peas. Included was a beaker of rice wine delivered out of a wooden barrel with a ladle.

The band also performed a marching display and concert for the local residents in town.

Aberdeen fishing village was another interesting place to visit, with its Junks, Sam pans and floating restaurants. It was, however, extremely overcrowded with the families who lived on their boats, named the Tanka, or boat people. The conditions were very unhygienic and from a policing point of view hard to control.

Junks in Aberdeen Harbour

Aberdeen was used as a typhoon shelter and in times of emergency, pleasure craft, sampans and junks were crowded into the harbour to such an extent that the fire breaks got congested, leaving no space for the emergency services to get through. This was a major problem for the marine authority and the police had to regularly move, by force, if necessary, some craft to other designated storm shelters around the Island.

Our two-week visit to Hong Kong went by very quickly, and soon we were flying out, weaving through the tower blocks of Kowloon and back to the UK. What an experience! The first of many I was going to encounter with the Band of the Grenadier Guards.

The one souvenir I was able to stow in my suitcase. An oil painting by Patrick Lee.

Oil painting by Patrick Lee

Chapter 6

No sooner had we arrived back in England and I was preparing for the most important day of my life.

Mary, my childhood sweetheart, and I had planned to get married earlier on in February of that year, but had to cancel through what was called the exigencies of the service. We lost deposits on hiring a hall and on hiring in caterers and so on 21st February 1976 we got married on a shoe string budget, and it was fantastic!

Mr & Mrs Spencer- 21st February 1976

Mary wore a dress borrowed from a relative, spending £2.50 getting it dry-cleaned, and I wore my uniform.

My best man was my twin brother Terry and my ushers were friends of mine from the band and from Kneller Hall. My professor, Paul Harvey and the London Saxophone Quartet performed and our Chauffeur was a trombonist from the band. He also worked for an undertaker, and so our car was a gleaming vintage Austin Princess. Our wedding breakfast consisted of all sorts of goodies, both in food and liquid form provided by relatives.

At the end of the afternoon, we were driven down to Rye in Sussex for our honeymoon at the Mermaid Inn. On the first night we had a marvellous meal in their restaurant, followed by after dinner drinks sitting by the giant fireplace. On retiring to our room with a four-poster bed in it, I switched off the radio. Suddenly the radio crackled into life. "Do you require room service Sir?".

After we came back from our honeymoon and my two weeks leave, to the hilarity of the band, I ended up in Millbank Military Hospital in London for a hernia repair. In actual fact, my appointment had been planned for some time, but the band members did not see it that way.

I reported back to the band after a further two weeks sick leave to find we had a new boss. Major Peter Parkes became the Director of Music of the Royal Army Medical Corps Band. Whilst awaiting our new director, Lt. Col. Rodney

Bashford had been brought back out of retirement to take the reins.

Col. Rodney was a highly respected conductor, arranger and composer and was universally loved by members of the band and indeed the whole regiment. On and off parade he was to be seen immaculately dressed in either uniform or pin striped suit. He also had a great rapport with the band. On one occasion, we were in the chapel at Chelsea Barracks, our band practice room, for our last rehearsal in preparation for the Christmas morning service in the Guards Chapel. As usual, as Rodney walked in we all stood smartly to attention. He was suited and booted, wearing a bow tie. He immediately espied Jim Beryl, one of our percussionists, also wearing a bow tie, but his was of the Christmas variety, with flashing lights on it. There was silence and then Rodney said "Yes Beryl and I bet it spins around too". As if by obeying an order the offending bow tie did indeed spin around. Again there was silence by all assembled awaiting to see what Rodney's reaction would be. There was just the slightest smirk on his face as he said "Well done Beryl" "Be seated Gentlemen, let's make this rehearsal brief, then we can get to the Rising Sun for a Christmas pint!"

Jim Beryl was one of many great characters in the band. On another occasion we were in St Pol Sur Mer, Calais as the exhibition band for a marching band festival. As such, we had to march through the town a number of times during the day. On the last march of the day, we had to march down the main road and form up outside the Mairie to greet the town mayor. As we were about to step off, Col. Rodney was heard saying "Where's Beryl?" He was missing from the band. We carried on without him to get to the town hall on time. We saw the mayoral procession coming towards us. The mayor was seated in an open topped Rolls-Royce and next to him waving to us and the assembled crowds, with a cigar in one hand and a glass of champagne in the other, resplendent in his scarlet tunic and bearskin was Jim Beryl. Col. Rodney just very quietly said "When we get back home, lock him up Band Sgt Major." Yet again you could see that wry smile on his face as he saw the funny side of it. Jim was just let off with a mild reprimand.

We said our farewells to Col. Rodney early in 1977 and another fine musician and conductor was appointed to be our new Director of Music. Captain Derek Kimberley. Just in time for our next adventure abroad.

Chapter 7

1977 was going to be a very busy year. Captain Kimberley had just arrived as our new Director of Music in time for the celebrations of Her Majesty the Queen's Silver Jubilee. The most important parade for us was the Queen's Birthday Parade, Trooping the Colour. Arrangements started quite early in the year. The music had to be chosen and this was done by the bands playing a selection of music in front of the Major-General Sir John Swinton, KCVO OBE with the Brigade Major and the Garrison Sergeant Major Alec Dumon Coldstream Guards, or affectionately known as Black Alec when out of earshot.

We also had a week known as "Spring Drills" where we were rifted around the square by eager and in our eyes over enthusiastic Drill Sergeants. At the end of this week the band had to be inspected by the Regimental Adjutant, finishing with a march past with him taking the salute. Once this had all been done, there was the Major General's inspection, with us in our best scarlet and gold tunics with gleaming brasses and boots and with bearskins immaculately groomed. Anyone picked up for any imperfection knew they were in for big trouble. The Major General was not such a problem, it was the seemingly endless entourage of officers following him. I remember one such occasion where a young officer stood in front of me and said in a very plummy voice "I say, do you really need to wear spectacles?" As tradition dictates in the Grenadier Guards, I was not allowed to answer either in the affirmative or in the negative and so I just had to say "Sir". I remember another inspection where the musician standing next to me, Vic Watley, was picked on by another young officer, who unfortunately had a terrible stutter. "I,I,I s, say, do your B,bboots need to go go to the boot repairers?" Vic being very quick witted, promptly replied "Cobblers Sir."

With all of this completed, the massed bands rehearsals started, under the eagle eyed "Black Alec". The massed bands in 1977 consisted of more than four hundred musicians led by five drum majors. The most complex manoeuvre for the bands to rehearse was the "Spin Wheel".

Lt. Col. Rodney Bashford described it thus. "A 'wheel' is not an easy manoeuvre with even a small body of troops, and with a block of 400 men the normal wheel is impossible. The massed band therefore pivots on its own centre, so that certain outer ranks and files march long distances in a hurry while the centre and inner ranks loiter with extreme intent, or merely mark time. Yet others not only step sideways but back- wards as well. This highly complex movement is called a 'spin-wheel', the details of which can be found in no drill book or manual of ceremonial. Its complexity defies description, and if the truth were known, many of the participants know not whither they go or, on arrival, how they got there. The spin-wheel is almost an art form and each performance of it, although similar in essentials, is different in detail. Most of the performers are adjusting their actions to suit the needs of the spin-wheel of the moment, having adjusted their movements quite otherwise on other occasions."

"The public is, hopefully, unaware of all this, and unless forewarned will likely as not miss the action completely, for it all looks so simple and inevitable from a spectator's seat. The public is, also hopefully, unaware of events in the epi-centre of that elegantly spinning body of men. The spectator hears only the music, but those on parade in the vicinity of the spin-wheel are aware of the deafening cacophony of crotchets and quavers plus much shouting and gesticulating as the five directors of music, hidden within the ranks, and the senior NCOs bid to control the wanderings of the less experienced brethren, lost to the world in what to them must resemble a super-orchestrated fairground roundabout gone mad. And as this spinning, roaring mass slowly gains equi-librium the raw ones are suddenly, frighteningly conscious of something amiss, a slight miscalculation perhaps on someone's part, for half the band is facing north, and the other south. Then a distant, ghostly scream, seemingly ema-nating from a euphonium to the north, effects an about turn by the eastern half. And all is finished."

Paul Harvey, my professor, from Kneller Hall once spoke to me about his time with the Band of the Irish Guards during National Service. On his first troop he was positioned next to his Director of Music, the legendary Lt. Col. 'Jiggs' Jaeger. During the spin wheel Paul marched off in the wrong direction and found himself in the Scots Guards Band. He was then promptly directed back to his place next to Jiggs who just turned to him and said "Welcome home Harvey." Other rehearsals for the troop included "Trooping Guards" where mini troop rehearsals were combined with Changing the Guard. Also, two full dress rehearsals, the Major General's review, the following week would be the Colonel's Review and then finally, Trooping the Colour itself. In May and June of that year we carried on with the usual annual events such as the Beating the Retreat on Horse Guards and playing on the bandstand at the Chelsea Flower Show. Between 6th and 12th June the band were involved in many events, in London and Windsor to celebrate the Silver Jubilee of her Majesty the Queen.

Rehearsals had also started for The Silver Jubilee Tour of the United States and Canada as well as producing an LP for the tour.

And so on 20th September 1977 we flew by a Pan Am 747 Jumbo jet into JFK airport, New York, to embark on my first major tour of North America. A tour that would last three months, performing in fifty-six cities. A tour where I would experience all four seasons travelling approximately anti-clockwise around the United States and Canada.

Waiting at JFK for us were the two Greyhound buses to take us to the Abbey Victoria Hotel, known locally as the Shabby Abbey, but to us it seemed like a five star hotel, right in the middle of New York City on Seventh Avenue at 51st Street. A journey that should have been very brief, except that there was a huge Gay rights march going on in the city that day.

For the next couple of days we had rehearsals at Madison Square Garden and at the World Trade Centre, plus many press calls, television and radio interviews. Finally, we moved off to Hartford Connecticut for our first concerts and again more interviews and receptions.

Band of the Grenadier Guards marching over the Brooklyn Bridge 1977. (The person wearing the Bearskin, second in from the right is me.)

On tour with us were the Pipes, Drums and Dancers of the1st Battalion, Scots Guards, under the direction of Pipe Major Slattery. Most of the band were accommodated on one bus, with a few band members on the other bus with the Scottish contingent. It was not long before there were complaints from many band members about the constant tap tapping on the practice pads of the drummers and the end- less low moan of the pipers' chanters in their endeavours for perfection, (which they undoubtedly achieved) as the miles went by.

Back to our first concerts. To start with I took a great interest in paper reviews and write ups, when there was time before moving off to our next location to get a newspaper. Some journalists were very imaginative and creative in their journalistic skills. I still have a paper cutting from Hartford, Friday 23 September, reporting on a rehearsal. "The dancers had been off their jigs all afternoon, even to the point where the sergeant in charge had to put the point of his sword under the nose of a recalcitrant dancer. "**PUT IN LINE!**" The reporter went on to say "The same sergeant later used a kidney punch to line up a balky dancer." This, of course, was all untrue. Even in the 1970s, particularly under the gaze of photographers and journalists, this would not have happened. Nevertheless, the following day we were given a very stern warning on how to behave in public and in particular in front of the members of the press.

And so after a couple of days rehearsing and performing in the provinces, working with the stage management team and the lighting technicians, we were ready to move back to New York and the Shabby Abbey, to play two nights at the iconic Madison Square Garden. The Garden first opened its doors in 1879 and has been the venue for many political, and sporting events, along with top music acts that included Elvis Presley, John Lennon, the Rolling Stones, Bob Dylan, Madonna, Elton John, Stevie Wonder, The Who, U2, Bruce Springsteen, and many more. And now us! We performed to a packed audience for two nights running at Madison Square Garden followed by a complete day off in New York to see the sights. I don't know how we fitted it all in, but we got around and up the Empire State Building, the World Trade Centre and of course the Statue of Liberty. We were also informed that if we went to the TKTS cabin on Times Square, we could get discounted tickets for Broadway shows. "A Chorus Line" was the choice for my room mate, Ken Jones and myself. The Tony and Pulitzer Prize-winning musical A Chorus Line, written by Marvin Hamlisch, began performances on Broadway at the Sam S. Shubert Theatre July 25, 1975. When it closed 15 years later on April 28, 1990, it was the longest-running show in Broadway history, having played 6,137 performances. What an experience! I had never seen a show like it, or the interaction that took place between the actors and the audience.

The next morning we were back on the road, performing in Poughkeepsie, Ottawa, Toronto and Buffalo, to name just a few of the venues. We soon got into a routine of arriving at an hotel or motel, collecting room keys and the all important mail from home, then going to the performance venue to rehearse, changing our sequences as required by the size of the arena or stage area. After our concerts, there were always many invites from societies to attend receptions. We were amazed at the hospitality given to us throughout the tour.

Some days we were travelling four or five hundred miles between towns and cities and so we had to load the coaches and set off promptly in the mornings, normally 8 am. Some found it more difficult to get "up and out" than others and so a dollar a minute fine was imposed on all late comers. The dollars collected were saved to fund an end of tour party in December. One occasion particularly sticks in my mind when we were sitting on the coach one morning awaiting our departure. We were missing one musician who will remain nameless here, who suddenly arrived in a sports car driven by a very attractive young lady. He was thirty minutes late. As he very shamefacedly got onto the coach, the whole band burst out into song. As was appropriate for the place we were just leaving the song was " I met a girl in Kalamazoo". I don't think he has ever lived that one down!

Our tour manager, Bill Mullaney, working for Columbia Artists, was a very affable man and ensured that everything ran as smoothly as possible and if there were any problems was capable of ironing things out with ease. He used to carry a cold box on our coach and on particularly long journeys would also act as "mine host" and offer gin and tonics

or equally chilled soft drinks to those who were around him
and still awake.

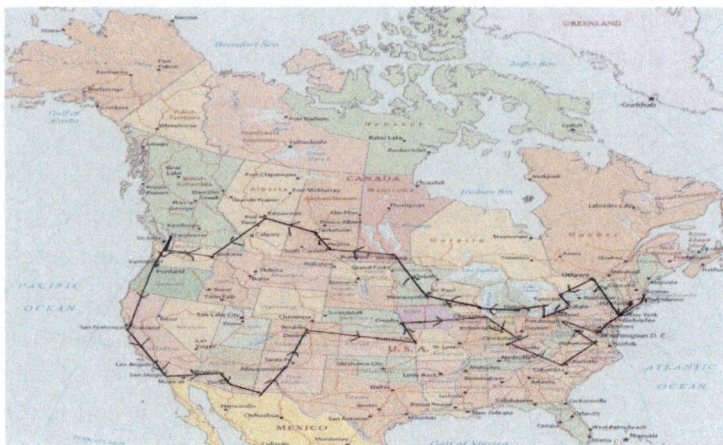

Tour of the United States and Canada 1977

Tony Sismundo was our driver, again a very friendly chap, a
New Yorker of Italian descent. He used to stay in touch with
other bus drivers and truckers on the road by means of CB
radio. This was extremely useful for getting travel news,
whether it be bad weather or road closures.

On one sleepy afternoon, travelling on a very long, straight
highway through the mid-West, Tony's radio crackled into
life and a woman's voice was to be heard. "Hey, if you
wanna good time, stop off at Junction 59." Tony replied,
"Lady, I have on board my bus the band of Her Majesty's
Grenadier Guards and they have been on tour for the last six
weeks." After what I think was a silence, summing up the

situation, the reply from the lady on the other end of the radio was "Jesus Christ, Drive On!"

Looking at the map of our tour, I now realise how fortunate we were. I first viewed the Northern Lights in Edmonton, Alberta, and whales off Vancouver. Moving south-wards, we had to visit Disneyland in Anaheim and we stayed for four nights in the Hollywood Roosevelt Hotel, right on the Boulevard. Hollywood was to be quite eventful. On one afternoon a group of us were having a little party in a room on the ground floor of the hotel when a man with a revolver climbed through the window, told us to lie on the floor, with our hands on our head, whilst he robbed us, then casually went out the way he came in. No one had a chance of catching him. It all happened so fast.

At one of our performances I met an American Marine Top Sergeant who said that he thought there might be someone that I would like to meet after the show. He took me to a bar in Downtown Hollywood, where he introduced me to Dean Martin. We spent a very jovial couple of hours, having a couple of beers and sharing anecdotes. On another evening a few of us were taken to a mansion in Beverly Hills. As we went in I was aware of many awards; Academy Awards, Emmy Awards and the Pulitzer Prize, for his work on "Chorus Line". I was in the house of, and being entertained by, the very man that wrote the show that I had seen a month previously on Broadway. Marvin Hamlisch.

On tour, many days were similar to one another. Morning checkout, travel maybe four or five hundred miles, check in to the next hotel, visit the arena or theatre, evening performance, attend a reception and finally go to bed. We generally had one day off every two weeks, although that could have been a travel day.

What interested me was the ever changing landscapes from cactus and desert, to mountainous regions with glorious flora and fauna, along with the change in regional clothing and dress, with men wearing Stetsons and elaborate leather boots. Many towns sold Indian jewellery, particularly using turquoise gem stones.

Our coach driver Tony Sismundo was a veteran of many years on performing arts tours and went out of his way to highlight various mountains and canyons for us to visit. He also had excellent knowledge of local restaurants and cuisine which we could visit when there was time.

There was quite a large contingent of the band who were Salvationists, and they were greeted by members of the Salvation Army wherever we went. Indeed my friend and roommate for the tour was Ken, also a Salvationist. In Saskatoon, Saskatchewan, Ken and myself were invited to a Brunch by a lovely Salvation army family. Making conversation during the meal, one of the rather attractive young daughters said "You must both be absoloutely exhausted from touring?" Ken replied "Well no, actually I feel quite perky." The young girl blushed and there was a long silence, until one of the older men in the room discreetly informed us that the word "perky in these parts means randy."

Earlier in the year, a group of Baptists from Kentucky came and visited our church, Emmanuel Baptist Church in Gravesend. As hosts, Mary and I showed a lovely couple, John and Louise Sandridge around the sights of London and some of the historic areas of where we lived in Kent. I told them that I would be visiting Kentucky on our forthcoming tour and suggested that perhaps we could meet up.

On Tuesday 15th November we were going to perform in Lexington, Kentucky and the previous evening we were in Cincinnati. John and Louise sent me an airline ticket so that I could fly to visit them in Louisville, and then they would drive me to Lexington for the evening performance.

I booked an early morning call at the reception of the Holiday Inn, in Cincinnati to catch my flight, but with all the excitement of this adventure, I was awake much earlier than the early call that I requested, which did not come. I went to reception to catch my airport taxi to find the reception staff bound and gagged. They had been robbed during the night. I unbound them and left them to call the police and I carried on with my journey.

I had a wonderful day in Kentucky. John and Louise took me to the Blue Grass horse auctions and to the racecourse, famed for the Kentucky Derby. I was also taken to the Heaven Hills Distillery, one of the first distilleries to make

Bourbon. My hosts were tee-total Baptists but they brought me here as reputedly it was a Baptist Minister, Elijah Craig who invented it. I didn't get to try the Bourbon, but I did get some Bourbon flavoured chocolates. Also on the day's agenda was lunch where I was served up a local dish of country baked ham with red eye gravy, grits and greens.

Then John and Louise got me to Lexington, well in time to prepare for yet another performance.

After this, we started moving northwards, through the Carolinas, Washington D.C. and finally Boston, before departing for home out of JFK Airport New York. Many, whom I toured with, if reading my epistle might say. "What about when that happened, or you missed out such and such." All I can say is there are so many fond memories and hilarious anecdotes that I could have included, that this book would have to be one huge volume on its own.

The band gave sixty-five performances with just ten rest days and stayed in fifty-one hotels or motels on our tour of North America. We landed back in the UK and Mary picked me up from Gatwick Airport. I think one of the first things I said to her was "I never want to see the inside of an hotel ever again." Little did I know that she had packed me a new set of clothing into our car for a couple of days, away at the Mermaid Hotel in Rye, Sussex.

Chapter 8

During the 1980s, the 2nd battalion Grenadier Guards were stationed in Munster as part of BAOR. Munster was a very interesting town. At its centre is St. Lambert's Church where three iron baskets hang from the tower. In 1536 these were used to expose the corpses of Jan van Leiden, Bernhard Krechting, and Bernhard Knipperdolling after they were publicly tortured and killed in the Prinzipalmarkt for leading the Münster Rebellion. On one occasion, a group of us attended a Weihnachtgesange concert in the church. It was freezing cold and I remember coming out of the building, just lit by candles, into the snow and bright lights of the Christmas Market, also to the sound of "German Beer Band" music and the smell of Glühwein.

The visits to both battalions were something we always looked forward to. Our musical duties were varied, from playing in the officer's and sergeant's messes for dinners, attending church services and marching on the parade square. Not forgetting playing for the battalion's wives clubs.

In Berlin we stayed with the 1st Battalion Grenadier Guards in Spandau Barracks, right next to the prison where Rudolph Hess was held. The band took part in the Berlin Tattoo, both in 1979 and 1981. Whilst in Berlin we joined up with the Pipes and Drums of the Scots Guards and recorded the first ever recording onto EP of "Highland Cathedral". We all thought it could be a hit and would sell many, many copies, but the powers that be thought differently, and it never went into production. Look how popular that tune is now, in so many different arrangements.

Whilst in Berlin, when not rehearsing and performing, we saw the sights of this amazing city and even went through "Checkpoint Charlie" and visited East Berlin. I actually went on even more of a sightseeing adventure. Early one morning I went out with a reconnaissance patrol, and under cover of darkness we drove into East Germany and observed, hidden and from a distance, Russian tank manoeuvres. Fortunately, I had my super eight movie camera with me and was able to capture everything on film. Goodness knows what would have happened if we had been captured.

On many occasions I had the opportunity to visit the Deutsche Oper, the Berlin opera House, and the Philharmonie, the famous Berlin Concert Hall. Some of us, dressed up in our number one uniforms went through Checkpoint Charlie to attend a performance at the Komische Oper in East Berlin. It was quite funny and obvious how we were being followed whilst walking through the streets from the Brandenburg Gate and down the Behrenstrase to where the opera house is located.

As well as playing within the regimental band, I also played clarinet in the orchestra, a small ensemble consisting of four violins, viola, cello and string bass, flute, oboe, clarinet, bassoon, plus trumpet, French horn, trombone and piano.

The orchestra was led by our Assistant Band Sergeant Major, a very fine violinist, Andy Teague.

Our main job was to play for investitures and state banquets at Buckingham Palace and for the presentation of Gold Awards at St. Jame's Palace. I always found it interesting viewing the proceedings and just generally "people watching" at these events, particularly viewing Her Majesty, The Queen, meticulously inspecting banqueting arrangements and His Royal Highness, Prince Philip, walking with his entourage through the rooms at St James Palace. As he passed us on his inspection he would always shout out, with a glint in his eye "MORNING SQUEAKERS AND SCRAPERS." Hence the title of this book. Of course, on cue, we were always expected to laugh. Prince Philip was the Colonel of the Grenadier Guards and took his duties very seriously. He visited the regiment frequently and indeed took a great interest in the band.

In the 1970s and 80s the band travelled extensively to the Netherlands and Belgium. The Regiment was first raised in 1665 by King Charles II in Bruges and was called "The Royal Regiment of Guards." This title was to remain until after the defeat of Napoleon in 1815 at Waterloo when the title was changed to "The First or Grenadier Regiment of Foot Guards." It was not surprising that we performed in Bruges, Brussels, Ghent and Wetteren. Many of the locals also remembered that it was, in part, the Guards Armoured Division that liberated them towards the end of the Second World War and the hospitality shown to us was amazing. It was nothing to march through Wetteren and stop at cafés to be offered glass upon glass of chilled Stella Artois and have dozens of Corps Diplomatique cigars thrust into our hands.

The Orchestra travelled by mini bus over to Brussels in June 1980 to play for a ball, held at the British Embassy, commemorating Belgium's 150th Anniversary. Princess Anne attended as the representative of the UK's Royal Family. Towards the end of that glittering evening, she came up to us and enquired if we knew how to play an eightsome reel? "Ay Ma'am, we can", replied our second violinist, Graham, a keen folk fiddler from Cumbria and with that he started to play. Within a matter of seconds we were all able to pick out the tune and the harmonies. Immediately Her Royal Highness picked out a partner to dance with and in minutes had, all around her joining in. It was a lovely evening. Princess Anne came and thanked us and we were all presented, by the embassy, with a bottle of Lanson Champagne with a specially printed label with the crossed flags of Belgium and the United Kingdom on it.

The next day was a rest day and the Burgermeister of Wetteren turned up in his Fire Chief's car to take a few of us back to his home town for the day, travelling with the siren blaring and the red light flashing, we did the some 49 kilometres in a matter of minutes.

The early 1980's was a time of immense happiness for me as well as that of great sadness. In 1980 our son Chris was born and our daughter, Helen came along in 1982. Both of whom have become fine musicians. Chris as a top clarinet-tist with the Band of the Scots Guards and Helen, a beauti-ful vocalist and is currently Head of Music at a British school in Abu Dhabi. They in turn have given us wonderful grandchildren.

My twin brother Terry, had been suffering with Non-Hodgkin's Lymphoma and passed away in 1981. To this day, there is hardly a day that I don't think about him.

That year my duties took me away to Berlin from 16th of September until the 7th October and to Munster from 7th December until 18th December. Between these dates the band were involved in public duties (Changing the Guard) in London and Windsor. On Saturday 10th October we were playing for the Guard Mounting Ceremony at Buckingham Palace. At the end of the parade, we were to march the old guard over to Wellington Barracks, to board military coaches to take us back to Chelsea Barracks. As we were about to proceed out of Buckingham Palace a signal was received to say that we should wait, as the Queen was just about to arrive and a Royal Salute had to be given. We then marched towards Wellington Barracks and saw the Tower of London Guard on their way to Chelsea. We got on our buses and followed theirs down towards Chelsea. Our buses were halted by the traffic lights by Victoria Bus Station, but the Irish Guards coach proceeded into Ebury Bridge road.

There was a huge explosion. A radio-controlled device had been set off. Sadly two civilians were killed and forty were injured including twenty three soldiers. Our driver was very quick thinking and we diverted right towards Sloane Square and into the back entrance to the barracks. A very sad day indeed. I believe that this was a sheer quirk of fate. If we had not been delayed by having to wait to play the Royal Salute, our coach, I believe, would have been ahead of the Tower of London guard's transport.

In November 1981 the band embarked on a very unique concert tour, which became an annual event for years to come. The show was called 'Tea and Trumpets'.

'Tea and Trumpets'

'Tea and Trumpets' was devised by Lt. Col. Kimberley, in conjunction with George Logan and Patrick Fyffe, otherwise know as Dr Evadne Hinge and Dame Hilda Bracket.

Hinge and Bracket were a couple of young men who dressed up as two elderly spinsters who had wonderful, imagined careers as classical singers. Dr. Evadne accompanied Dame Hilda on the piano. Our concerts consisted of singing and playing, with many funny stories and improvisations and of course, being drag artists, much double entendre.

Hinge and Brackett were the epitamy of comic actors and I used to watch in amazement as they would, time after time, rehearse their acts, on and off stage to attain perfection. They were also two of the nicest people you could meet. Years later, after I had left the band, they were performing in a double act show in Gravesend that I attended. Dame Hilda almost immediately spotted me in the audience and went into an improvised comedy story. "Have you heard the story about Tony Spencer and his pussy?" The audience loved the story and I think I laughed the loudest.

Dame Hilda and Dr. Evade made an appearance at the band's Tercentenary concert in the Royal Albert Hall on the 18th October 1985. The last performance of "Tea and Trumpets" was around Christmastime. They said farewell to us with a small present each and an invitation:

You are invited
to
Cocktails and other stories
in the circle bar
after the show

H & B   Admit one

Souvenir Programme

Chapter 9

By 1982 the band had relocated to Regents Park Barracks from Chelsea whilst awaiting the refurbishment of their new accommodation in Wellington Barracks and their purpose built rehearsal rooms. It was the year that we travelled to Edinburgh to take part in the spectacular Edinburgh Tattoo. The Edinburgh Tattoo in 1982 took place from August 6th to August 28th. Steve Hill and myself decided to share the journey up to Edinburgh with Graham Hetherington and persuaded him to hook up a trailer, so that we could also bring up our motorbikes. We knew that there would be many days of non-stop rehearsing, but once the shows started, there would be a fair bit of free time for sightseeing and that is where our motorbikes came in very handy. Steve and I were very fortunate for by this time we were both Sgts. Mess Members and were looked after very well in the Redford Barracks Sergeants Mess. I seem to remember there being a buffet or some form of entertainment when we returned after the show each evening. I don't think it was so comfortable for the other ranks. The barracks was built around the 1900s and the men were housed in a cramped barrack room. Of course, they made their own entertain-ment, but one evening someone was caught riding a bike down the middle of the barrack room by the duty piquet sergeant and promptly was locked up. This did not go down to well with morale.

I did manage to get a travel warrant for Mary, our two-year-old son, Chris and our three month old daughter, Helen to come by train to visit us for a long weekend during the tattoo. Of course being Edinburgh it rained non stop and we spent most of the time staying warm in front of the fire in our B&B accommodation, being looked after by a very kindly landlady, but for me it was a real treat. I had missed them so much.

Every evening we travelled a different route to and from Edinburgh Castle by coach. Security at that time was very tight due to what we now know as "The Troubles". There was a very severe threat of terrorist attacks by the IRA.

Just a week or so before going to Edinburgh, on 20th July 1982, I was with the band, playing for a memorial service for Lord Gort in St Paul's Cathedral. Lord Gort was a military leader who served in both the First and Second World Wars. He was awarded the Victoria Cross for his bravery in the First World War and he played a major role in the evacuation of allied troops in the Second World War.

As usual, we arrived early at St Paul's to set up and have a rehearsal. At around 10.40 am we heard an explosion. Little did we know, but on that horrific morning, two bombs detonated by the IRA were to cause carnage in London. The first blast, in Hyde Park, killed two cavalrymen and injured twenty-three others. Seven horses were also killed or had to be put down because of their horrific injuries.

A second bomb was detonated under the bandstand in Regents Park at 12.55 pm whilst the Band of the 1st Battalion Royal Green Jackets were giving a lunchtime concert; killing seven musicians and injuring a further twenty-four.

When we came out of St Paul's there were police everywhere and some with sniffer dogs were closely examining our coach. Finally, we were allowed onto the coach and had a police escort back to Regent's Park barracks. A couple of police officers travelled with us on the coach and informed us of what had happened. There was an uneasy silence from us all with the realisation of what had happened that morning and of course, the possibilty that it could have happened to us.

Arriving back we were confined to the barracks for the afternoon. The Royal Green Jackets Coach was brought into barracks for safekeeping. We searched it for other devices and kept a watching brief on it.

We were dismissed to return to our loved ones at around 6.00 pm. All with heavy hearts, our thoughts with those at Hyde Park who were just carrying out ceremonial duties, mainly for the tourists who flock to London throughout the year to enjoy the spectacle. Also, thinking about our brother musicians in the Green Jackets who were, at the time, playing a selection from the musical "Oliver" for the enjoyment of visitors and office workers alike taking a lunch time break. Many lives were changed from that day onwards.

Chapter 10

In November 1982 the first Battalion Grenadier Guards were deployed to Cyprus for a short six-month tour.

The Turkish army had invaded Cyprus in 1974, splitting the Island in half and declaring the North of the Island a separate independent state with the south of the Island governed by the Greeks. A buffer zone between both factions was created across the Island, dividing the capital, Nicosia in half.

The battalion was divided into two. One half providing support for the United Nations peace keeping force on the buffer, zone, or the green line as it was known, whilst the other halves' duties was the security of the Sovereign base area with its headquarters at Alexander Barracks, Dhekelia.

On 8th February 1983 the band flew out from Brize Norton on a RAF VC10 and in a matter of hours landed at RAF Akrotiri and then onward to Dhekelia to pay a visit to the battalion. Our duties as usual were varied, and we possibly saw more of Cyprus than many that were on a posting there. The reason being, that other contingents of the peace keeping force requested that we visit them to play for a parade or a reception. We were afforded great hospitality on these visits and the Danish, Swedish, Finnish contingents come immediately to mind. We got quite accustomed to feasting on smorgasbord.

Part of our stay was at the Sovereign Base in Dhekelia. There were some amusing things to get used to as musicians coming into the environment of battalion life. One morning, having breakfast in the cookhouse, the Officer of the Day entered and asked "Any complaints?" One naïve, young musician promptly answered "Sir, there's no marmalade." The officer was accompanied by a very burly Sergeant in waiting, who had no hesitation in his response. "LOCK HIM UP!!!!!!!"

We did get some free time in Dhekelia and one morning Dave Craft and myself decided to make use of one of the sailing dinghies available to the regiment. No sooner had we pushed the boat down the ramp into the water than I felt what I thought was a rope tightening around my ankle. I stepped backwards out of the water to find the tentacles of a large octopus wrapped around it. I shook the creature off as quickly as I could and attempted a re-launch. The same thing happened again and again. We decided to abandon the idea of going sailing, there wasn't much breeze after all. We took the unfortunate cephalopod to a beach restaurant where Chef prepared it for our lunch. We could only imagine that the octopus had become attracted to the colour of my trainers.

Halfway through our tour of Cyprus the band moved to Nicosia. We all wondered what accommodation we might have? We knew that the Canadian UN contingent were billeted in one of the best hotels in town. Where were we to be housed? In Stone huts at Nicosia Airport. Each morning we

71

were issued with a ration of paraffin for our oil stoves. It was very cold in Cyprus in February and most mornings we awoke to a covering of snow, although it would normally have melted by lunchtime.

A few of us decided to hire a car and in our free time would go sightseeing, driving up into the Troodos Mountains or exploring the ancient city of Paphos with its ancient links to Aphrodite and Aphrodite's steps, where in mythology she stepped out of the sea. We also visited St. Paul's pillar where he was bound and tortured. According to the Acts of the Apostles St. Paul visited Cyprus along with Barnabas in 45AD to spread the word of Christianity. Cyprus became the first country in the world to be ruled by a Christian, Sergius Paulus.

We also visited the many Roman ruins in the area and the breathtakingly beautiful amphitheatre, Kourion, built on the cliffs overlooking the sparkling Mediterranean.

Walking through the buffer zone into the Turkish part of Nicosia was also on the agenda. The Ledra street crossing takes you right into the old part of the city. The sights and sounds were amazing. The smell of the Turkish coffee and the cooking coming from the numerous cafés; the sounds of the animals in the market place. We even witnessed the Halal slaughter of a goat as we passed through.

On visiting the mosque we were told to take our shoes off before entering. I was concerned that our shoes would be stolen. However, the elderly gentleman at the entrance informed us that our shoes would not be taken as Allah sees all and anyway if a thief was to be caught, "We cut their Fxxxxxx hands off".

Our final performing engagement was a parade that took place at Nicosia airport organised by Lt. Col Denison-Smith for those receiving the United Nations Peace- Keeping Medal. Two hundred and sixteen service men and women and seven police officers all told.

The band on parade at Nicosia airport

Back in Akrotiri we awaited our comfortable flight home After a long delay we were informed that we were flying home courtesy of a Hercules transporter that had been involved in the Beirut airdrop that day. After being issued with ear defenders, we were led onto the aircraft. Our seating was netting put over a bar on both sides of the aircraft with all the freight in the middle. Some of us climbed up the netting to sit on top of the freight, which was a little more comfortable. After a very long flight we eventually landed not at Brize Norton, but at RAF Lyneham in Wiltshire, to be followed by a long coach journey back to London.

What a wonderful adventure was our tour to Cyprus. The next couple of years was to take the Band of the Grenadier Guards to more far-flung places around the world and further exciting adventures...

Chapter 11

1984 saw the band travel a little closer to home to the Netherlands to perform in the Breda Military Tattoo. Security was very tight at this time and our accommodation was in a conscripts barracks, deep in a forest just outside Breda, with Dutch special branch officers accompanying us.

Food in the cookhouse was very basic with whatever was left over from lunch, turned into soup for tea. We slept on straw palliasses and after the first nights sleep many of us discovered that we had been attacked by bed bugs.

As usual we all made the best of our trip, visiting The Hague, Amsterdam and a place that was popular with the band, Scheveningen, a seaside resort, also extremely popular with topless bathers. Not that any of us noticed of course.

On 7th June of that year a regimental garden party was held at Burton's Court and Mary and I were greatly honoured by being presented to our Colonel in Chief, Her Majesty the Queen.

A very proud occasion for both of us

Later on that year the band took to its secondary role as medical assistants. We were involved from 15th September to 5th October in the largest ever British Army exercise and the biggest mobilisation since the Second World War, Operation Lionheart.

The band packed away their instruments and ceremonial uniforms and instead, searched the back of their lockers for combat uniforms, respirators and NBC suits (Nuclear, Chemical and Biological protection)

We flew out to RAF Gutersloh in Germany and then on to Menden by coach. Our first job was to set up a field hospital, spending hours filling up sandbags and then erecting the huge tents that were to be the various wards of the hospital. Within days we were joined by the doctors, nurses and auxiliaries that made up 201(Northern) General Field Hospital, RAMC. The hospital set up a triage system, so there was a reception ward to assess the severity of the patients' wounds, then, the general wards and lastly the evacuation ward.

Very soon the casualties started arriving and had to be dealt with. Our job, as medical assistants was to act as stretcher bearers, obtain and distribute supplies and generally assist the nursing staff.

I was assigned to the evacuation ward. After just a couple of days, the captain in command of the ward was suddenly called back to the UK and as the sergeant I was temporarily put in charge. I actually remained in charge for the duration of the exercise. Our job was to assess and evacuate our casualties and pass them on to a general hospital, or if fit enough, back to their unit. Most were notional, although we did have the occasional genuine casualty. At the height of the exercise we were evacuating hundreds per day. I remember one American GI turning up. We didn't know where to send him and he didn't know either, so he just made himself right at home on a camp bed in the corner of the ward and there he stayed.

I mainly worked the night shift. I found it was very strange having breakfast before getting some sleep and on awakening to have dinner. If we had a quiet night, I used to send my men to the morgue to get a bit of shut-eye (and then sleep the sleep of the dead.)

Sergeant Spencer taking a quick break to write home in full NBC kit

Menden was a lovely German town and its first churches were built in the 9th Century. News got to the surgeon commanding our hospital that an organist at one of these churches had collapsed with a heart attack and there was no one to play for the daily mass. I was asked if I could play for mass a couple of times a week. A job I very gladly took on. My final duty as an organist was to play for a service in the Garrison Church. I was very moved that the locals presented me with a beautiful hand painted, crystal beer glass, which I still treasure to this day.

Working in a field hospital was completely alien to me, but it was an amazing experience, particularly managing the wonderful men and women I had with me on the Evac Ward.

Chapter 12

1985 marked the tercentenary of the formation of the band and as such was celebrated towards the end of an very busy year.

Firstly however, the band paid a visit, in January, to the 2nd Battalion Grenadier Guards in Belize. As usual, they extended the greatest hospitality towards us and when we arrived at Airport Camp just outside Belize city the Sgt's Mess put on a fabulous barbecue for us. We were very well fed and the ice cold "Beliken" beer went down very well in the incredible heat, but the mess had arranged another form of entertainment for us.

Suddenly running around where we were sitting on rattan chairs, young ladies, heavily made up and wearing little girl's party frocks were laughing and screaming, with the intention of sitting on our laps and putting their arms around us. I can, to this day, still smell the aroma of cheap scent and BO that emanated from them. Raul's Rose Garden was a brothel located in Ladyville on the outskirts of Belize City and the Sgt's Mess had hired the girls for the afternoon for our amusement. Everyone had great fun, but was minded of the dangers of too much fraternisation with them on the briefings we had prior to our arrival.

Sgt Spencer searching for that ancient Mayan temple

We of course were visiting the battalion to work and we played for mess dinners, parades and concerts. We also performed two concerts in Belize City for the locals who seemed to enjoy our varied repertoire from "Light Cavalry" to "Carribean Cameo."

Belize City in 1985 was mainly shops and houses built of wood and corrugated iron, with mud roads and pathways. One morning it had been raining and as I walked along the High Street, I observed a congress of land crabs intent on crossing the road. Suddenly, like something out of a horror story, but with a hint of comedy, cars were running over them. The result being that vehicles were skidding and colliding into each other, even crashing into shops. Apparently this was quite a regular event.

Whilst staying at Airport Camp we met up with the Belizean Defence Force Band. Later in the year, Her Majesty the Queen was to pay her first ever visit to the country and our job was to give some sectional and full band rehearsals to this band in enabling them to play the National Anthem correctly on her arrival.

Sgt Spencer in Tropical Whites

After a week at Airport Camp the band travelled to Punta Gorda, close to the Guatemalan border where half the Battalion were serving with Battle Group South, patrolling the border and manning observation posts. To get there a few travelled by Puma helicopter, but for the rest of us it was a ten hour journey by RPL (Ramp Powered Lighter), crewed by men of the RCT maritime section.

For those stuck on the landing craft deck it was a very uncomfortable journey, with just a view of the blue sky and the blazing sun. I was very fortunate to be able to be in an elevated position on the bridge and was able to take in splendid views of the Belizean coastline.

A Ramp Powered Lighter

We performed to the troops in Punta Gorda and Rideau camp, just down the road, but most peculiarly we were escorted through the jungle to give a concert to a local tribe, descended from the Maya Indian civilization. We played our first piece of music and there was an eerie silence, but once our audience learnt how to applaud, there was no stopping them. They even started dancing and I think their favourite number was a selection of Michael Jackson's hits.

The band in concert at Punta Gorda

Whilst down in Punta Gorda we had the opportunity to travel by log canoes, powered by Yamaha outboard motors to one of the Cays lying off the mainland. Here we went fishing, snorkelling and generally having a chilled out time. I dived for Conch and used the meat extracted from its shell as bait. Fishing with a hand line, I caught a small blue shark which seemed to snap away at our feet until we got back on land. The local men who skippered our canoes were happy to eat it, whilst we dived for lobster, wrapped them in coconut palm leaves and barbecued them over driftwood.

Time to relax

Close by Punta Gorda was the Rio Grande river, another opportunity for a swimming and barbecue excursion in a jungle setting. Whilst swimming one had to be mindful of the snakes curled up on branches overhanging the sides of the river. There was also the strange sensation of the fish in the water, who, it was said, were related to the Pirahna. They didn't bite, but they could give you a nasty suck.

Away from the main body of swimmers, there was a cave to investigate. It was very slippery and our guides informed us that this was guano from the bats that dwelt inside.

Investigating a cave

Down river, I observed a small group of women making bread. They were kneading their dough, mixing corn flour with river water and occasionally, spitting into it to moisten it further, before cooking it over an open fire.

Now back with the swimming party, I spied another group of our intrepid explorers coming to join us and eating something. "Did you see that group of women?" "Ever so friendly they were." "They gave us some bread to eat, it's not bad. Do you want to try some?" "No thanks," was my quick response.

On another walk into the jungle from Rideau camp on a quest to find an ancient Mayan temple, Mick Stainer and I passed an old yellow American school bus with a sheeted awning over one side. Nearby an old Rastafarian looking man was digging. We said good morning, left him to his task and carried on our way. On our return, we saw that he had beautifully cultivated a square metre or two of land and was lying back, cross-legged on a deck chair, smoking a very long reefer. "What are you growing?" I enquired, to which he just replied "Grass man, grass!"

American school bus dwelling

The extreme poverty of the people of Belize was clear to see, but we were greeted with great friendliness wherever we went. It was nothing to see men, women and children, who having shaken iguanas out of trees, were then carrying them back home on what looked like dairy yokes across their shoulders for something to eat for dinner, or probably their only meal of the day.

Things have greatly changed in Belize since 1985. It now has a thriving tourist industry with luxurious holiday resorts and with fantastic new highways to travel, North, South, East and West of the country.

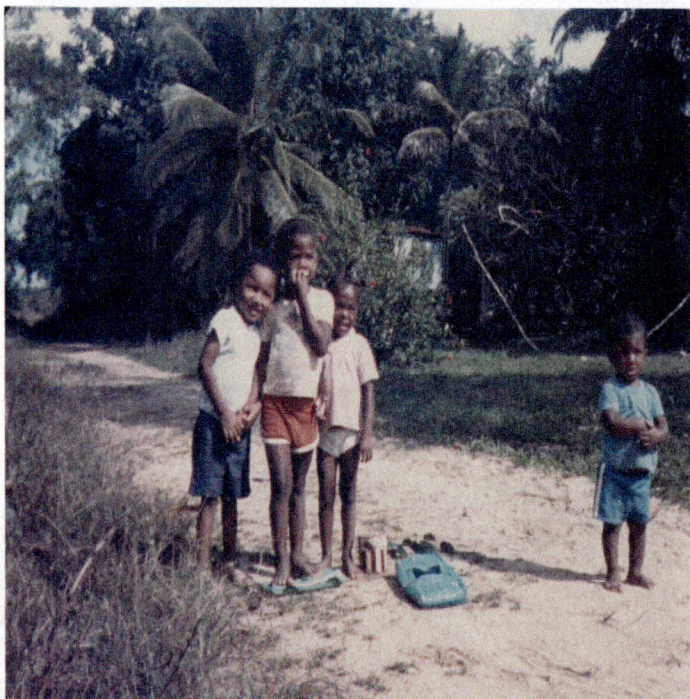

I made new friends

These were some of the Belizean dwellings that I saw back in 1985.

Belizean dwellings

We arrived back in the UK in February, but four days later than expected. We took off from Belize International Airport on an evening flight to Dulles International, Washington, to change cabin crew for our onward journey to Brize Norton. After a couple of hours, Graham, who had been watching the stars, informed me that the aircraft had in actual fact, turned around. Within minutes the Captain informed us that Dulles Airport was closed due to a heavy snow, and instead we were going to land in Jacksonville, Florida.

The Captain organised accommodation for all of us in a motel nearby and we would have to stay in Florida until the relief crew arrived to fly us home. Suddenly we had an all expenses paid holiday, courtesy of the Ministry of Defence American Express Card that he carried for such emergencies. A fitting end, we thought to a fantastic trip, before going back to the normal routine of band duties, annual weapon training.and of course the dreaded Spring drills, ensuring that we were up to standard for the upcoming Queen's Birthday Parade, Trooping the Colour.

Chapter 13

At the beginning of March the band embarked on a six week tour of Australia. We firstly performed at the Melbourne Military Tattoo as part of the 150th anniversary of the state of Victoria. It was here that I met up with a musician from the Royal Australian Air Force Band, Billy Miles, who was to become a lifelong friend. Billy and his wife took me into their home on a farm just outside Melbourne for the duration of the Tattoo and afforded me the greatest hospitality. I was to meet up with Billy on other occasions of our tour. He eventually came back to the UK and became an "In Pensioner" at the Royal Hospital, Chelsea, where he was to become their drummer. Certainly Billy died with his boots on and was doing what he loved doing as he collapsed on a rehearsal for the Royal Hospital's Founders day Parade on 2nd June 2017

Prince Andrew, Duke of York, talking to Drummer Billy Miles at the Founder's Day Parade, 2015

From Melbourne, we flew to Sydney to take part in the Royal Agricultural Show. The Royal Show is one of the largest shows of its kind in Australia, indeed the world.

Here again we met up with the Air Force Band and also with the Sydney Police Force Band, who gave us an exhilarating fishing excursion down the Hawkesberry river. I'm not sure how many fish we caught, but many stubbies of beer were consumed, and we were greeted with the most amazing barbecue when we got back on to land.

After a few days holiday on the Gold Coast at Surfers Paradise, (it's a hard life in the Band of the Grenadier Guards) we flew up to Townsville to embark on the final stage of our Australian tour.

Although the tour was hectic, enough time was found to visit Bondi Beach and the occasional trip to view Australia's beautiful flora and fauna. The highlight of the tour for me was flying up to Cairns and visiting Green Island on the Great Barrier Reef and taking a trip on the Cairns to Kuranda Railway.

The Kuranda Scenic Railway is a spectacular journey comprising unsurpassed views of dense rainforest, steep ravines and picturesque waterfalls within the World Heritage listed Barron Gorge National Park.

The Band of the
GRENADIER GUARDS

Australian Tour 1985

Townsville
– Sound Shell
Tues 16th April 7.30pm

Rockhampton
– Music Bowl
Wed 17th April 7.30pm

Brisbane
– Lyric Theatre
Performing Arts Complex
Sun 21st April 7.00pm

Well, all good things come to an end and we arrived back in London in good time for the Queen's Birthday Parade and Beating Retreat on Horse Guards.

Only a week after taking part in "The Trooping of the Colour", we were flying out to join other musicians in Berlin to perform a "Grand Military Concert" at the Wald-buhne, an arena close to the Olympic Stadium. The concerts took place from 25th to 30th June. Fifteen bands from the UK took part as well as the Berlin Brigade United States Command Band and 46 Regiment d'Infanterie Francaise. Also performing was the world famous Morriston Orpheus Choir. All under the direction of our boss, Lt. Col Derek Kimberley.

The Waldbuhne arena

No sooner had we returned to London than we were plunged directly into rehearsals for the Royal Tournament. The band formed the backbone of the massed bands and as befitted the Tercentenary Theme, a giant replica of the regi-mental drum formed the centrepiece of the arena backdrop.

The climax for our 300th Birthday Celebrations took place at the Royal Albert Hall on Friday 18th October.

Sharing the stage with us were The Royal Military Band of the Netherlands, The Royal Choral Society, and the Canoldir Male Voice Choir, with a special guest appearance from Dame Hilda and Dr. Evadne.

Sergeant Tony Spencer performing at the Royal Albert Hall, 18th October 1985

The line-up of guest conductors was equally illustrious, numbering among them, ex Grenadier Directors of Music, Lt. Col. Fred Harris O.B.E. and Lt. Col Rodney Bashford.

I had the privilege of being the clarinet soloist in the "Theme and Variations from La Traviata by Lovreglio." The sound of the resounding applause from a packed Albert Hall audience at the end of my performance is a sound that will remain with me for the rest of my life.

The concert proved to be a complete success and was recorded by the BBC for a Radio 2 broadcast and a record of the concert was also produced.

The night after the concert, a reunion dinner was held, where serving members mingled with their predecessors, some of whom had served in the band forty or more years ago. Colonel Duncan L.V.O. O.B.E. the Lieutenant Colonel commanding the regiment was amongst our special guests on the top table, and our guest speaker was the conductor, Ian Sutherland, otherwise known as "Musician Rafferty" when he was with the band.

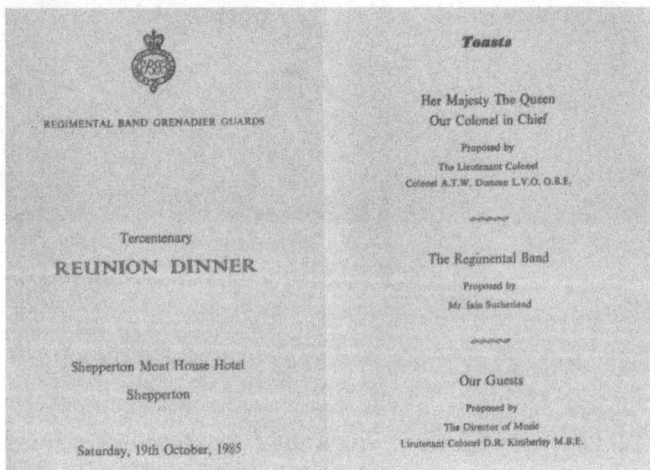

REGIMENTAL BAND GRENADIER GUARDS

Tercentenary
REUNION DINNER

Shepperton Moat House Hotel
Shepperton

Saturday, 19th October, 1985

Toasts

Her Majesty The Queen
Our Colonel in Chief
Proposed by
The Lieutenant Colonel
Colonel A.T.W. Duncan L.V.O. O.B.E.

The Regimental Band
Proposed by
Mr. Iain Sutherland

Our Guests
Proposed by
The Director of Music
Lieutenant Colonel D.R. Kimberley M.B.E.

My wife, Mary, had the honour of presenting a small memento to Lieutenant Colonel and Mrs. Kimberley on this special occasion. Our 300th year drew to a close with the band performing public duties over Christmas at Windsor Castle.

Chapter 14

In 1986 and 1987 the band visited both the 1st and 2nd Battalions of the regiment in Munster, serving as part of B.A.O.R., the British Army of the Rhine and also in Ballykelly, Northern Island. As I have said earlier in this book, it was always a pleasure to visit our battalions, playing for parades and giving concerts to the men and their families. Also, visiting local schools and generally performing in the local vicinity. These visits also gave us a better understanding of the tasks the men had to do, away from performing public duties in London and Windsor.

The year 1987 was significant for all of us serving in the Band of the Grenadier Guards. Most importantly with the retirement of our Director of Music Lt. Col. Derek Kimberley M.B.E. He had led the band for ten years and had taken us on tour all around the world. He was not only a fine conductor, composer and arranger, but also had the amazing ability to work out the most complex musical, marching displays.

Who would have thought that you could march and play to Puccini's "Humming Chorus", or to Shostakovich's "Festive Overture"? We didn't, but incredibly, it worked. So it was with sad hearts that we said farewell to Col. Derek and welcomed Major Rodney Parker as our new Director of Music, just in time for yet another tour of North America.

1987 saw the usual routine Spring drills in preparation for the Queen's Birthday Parade, weapon training and catching up on our medic skills in the event of being mobilized in our Field Hospital role.

The Queen's Birthday Parade (Trooping the Colour) in 1987 was held on Saturday 13th June. The previous year, Her Majesty rode on to parade, resplendent in her Scots Guards uniform on her mount, Burmese. From this year on, things were to be slightly different and she was driven in an open top carriage without uniform. The parade, of course, was no less special as we still had our Colonel on Parade.

A week prior to the "Troop", we travelled north to the Yorkshire TV studios to appear on "The Birthday Show". The band were delighted to be appearing with the page three model and pop singer, Samantha Fox, and of course treated her royally. During the Summer we also performed at a very wet Chelsea Flower Show and a very hot Henley Regatta.

Moving north again for the Great Yorkshire Show at Harrogate. I remember that on one wet afternoon at the show ground, the main arena was terribly waterlogged and to our horror over the tannoy came the announcement, "Ladies and Gentlemen, due to the inclement weather, the display by the Masters, Horses and Hounds of the Quorn Hunt has been cancelled. Instead, please welcome into the arena, the Band of the Grenadier Guards." With that we stepped off, marching on to a lake of around a foot deep of muddy water.

More exciting adventures were to ensue. Our last "Gig" before going on annual Summer leave was to Beat Retreat on the flight deck of the aircraft carrier, HMS Illustrious at Portsmouth. The Officers and men of this great ship gave us a full tour and afforded us great hospitality.

Moving from a huge ship, we then moved on to Guernsey for a week to play at the World Power Boat Championships. A few of us were lodging at Bordeaux Bay and hired a car from St Peter's Port for the duration of our trip. Unbelievably, driving to our "digs", we got lost and found ourselves at a pub somewhere in the middle of the island. On entering this hostelry we came upon a gentleman, surrounded by a bevy of beautiful young ladies. To our amazement, it was the actor and film star, Oliver Reed, who had no hesitation in inviting us to have a pint with him.

As I have mentioned earlier, we were to embark on another tour of North America. ten years on from my first trip. And so, for me, I had come a full circle. Rehearsals started in September. The band were accompanied on this tour the Drums and Pipes and Dancers of the Gordon Highlanders.

The tour was not the holiday that some may like to believe. We left London for Heathrow on 4th October and arrived back in London on 16th December. The band gave 62 performances in 59 cities in the United States and Canada. We travelled 21,000 miles of which 14,000 were by Greyhound Bus. 235 hours were spent on the buses. We stayed in 53 different hotels in 33 states and 3 Canadian Provinces. We were snowbound in Colorado, and sunburnt in Arizona. One of our buses was even struck by lightening in Sun City. We were travelling back through the desert to our hotel in Tucson, Arizona, when we encountered a storm, and a lightening bolt hit the air conditioning system of the pipers' coach. Fortunately no one was hurt, but we, on the band bus, found it very funny to see the pipers evacuating their smoke filled coach. We all considered it divine retribution for all the constant noise they had been making on the move, tapping on their drum practise pads and the constant low moans of their chanters.

The tour was an unforgettable experience, but ten years on from my first tour, it was one I would not wish to do again.

NORTH AMERICAN TOUR 1987

Oct. 7 Hanover, NH 603-646-3422 Rupert C. Thompson Arena	Oct. 28 Tempe, AZ 602-965-3434 Gammage Center	Nov. 13 Ogden, UT 801-626-6800 Weber State College	Dec. 1 Rochester, NY 716-546-2030 Rochester War Memorial
Oct. 8 Burlington, VT 802-656-3085 Patrick Gymnasium	Oct. 29 Sun City West, AZ 602-975-1900 Sundome Center for the Perf. Arts	Nov. 15 Denver, CO 303-573-7151 Denver Coliseum	Dec. 2 Syracuse, NY 315-424-8210 Onondaga County War Memorial
Oct. 9 Schenectady, NY 518-346-6204 Proctor's Theatre	Oct. 30 San Diego, CA 619-224-4176 San Diego Sports Arena	Nov. 17 Omaha, NE 402-342-7107 Omaha Civic Arena	Dec. 3 Storrs, CT 203-486-4228 Jorgensen Auditorium
Oct. 10 West Point, NY 914-938-4159 Eisenhower Hall	Oct. 31 Anaheim, CA 714-999-8980 2 perfs. Convention Center Arena	Nov. 18 Minneapolis, MN Check Local Listings	Dec. 4 Portland, ME 207-775-3458 Cumberland County Civic Center
Oct. 11 Fairfax, VA 703-432-0200 Patriot Center	Nov. 1 Los Angeles, CA 213-626-2953 Pauley Pavilion	Nov. 19 Milwaukee, WI 414-276-3300 Riverside Theatre	Dec. 5 Worcester, MA 617-755-6800 X50 The Centrum
Oct. 13 Richmond, VA 804-780-4970 Richmond Coliseum	Nov. 1 Pasadena, CA 818-304-8181 Pasadena Civic Auditorium	Nov. 20 Chicago, IL 312-922-2110 Auditorium Theatre	Dec. 6 Boston, MA 617-227-3200 Boston Gardens Arena
Oct. 14 Wilmington, NC 919-395-3042 Trask Coliseum	Nov. 3 Oakland, CA 415-639-7700 Oakland Coliseum	Nov. 21 Detroit, MI 313-567-6000 Cobo Arena	Dec. 8 Providence, RI 401-331-0081 Providence Civic Center
Oct. 15 Greensboro, NC 919-344-5546 Aycock Auditorium	Nov. 4 Sacramento, CA 916-922-7362 Arco Arena	Nov. 22 Jackson, MI 517-789-1600 Potter Center Music Hall	Dec. 9 Bethlehem, PA 215-867-8202 Stabler Arena
Oct. 16 & 17 Raleigh, NC 919-737-2836 William Neal Reynolds Coliseum	Nov. 5 Portland, OR 503-239-4422 Memorial Coliseum	Nov. 22 East Lansing, MI 517-355-6686 University Auditorium	Dec. 10 Hershey, PA 717-534-3911 Hershey Park-Arena
Oct. 18 Columbia, SC 803-777-2555 Carolina Coliseum	Nov. 6 Seattle, WA 206-628-0888 Seattle Coliseum	Nov. 24 Richfield, OH 216-659-9100 The Coliseum	Dec. 11 Baltimore, MD 301-347-2010 Baltimore Civic Center
Oct. 20 Asheville, NC 704-259-5771 Civic Center Arena	Nov. 7 Victoria, BC 604-384-1522 Memorial Arena	Nov. 25 Hamilton, ON 416-526-3000 Hamilton-Copps Arena	Dec. 12 Philadelphia, PA 215-336-3600 The Spectrum
Oct. 21 Nashville, TN 615-259-6217 Nashville Municipal Auditorium	Nov. 8 Vancouver, BC 604-280-4444 2 perfs. Agrodome	Nov. 26 Kitchener, ON 519-895-7125 Kitchener Memorial Auditorium	Dec. 13 Westbury, NY 516-333-0533 Westbury Music Fair
Oct. 22 Birmingham, AL 205-252-7548 Civic Center Concert Hall	Nov. 10 Walla Walla, WA 509-527-5157 Cordiner Hall	Nov. 27 Toronto, ON 416-977-1641 Maple Leaf Garden	Dec. 14 East Rutherford, NJ 201-460-4325 Byrne Meadowlands Arena
Oct. 23 Tupelo, MS Community Concerts Association	Nov. 11 Boise, ID 208-385-1766 Boise State University Pavilion	Nov. 28 Ottawa, ON 613-996-5051 Civic Center	
Oct. 24 Greenwood, MS 601-453-5636 Greenwood Leflore Civic Center	Nov. 12 Rexburg, ID 208-356-2230 Hart Auditorium	Nov. 29 Montreal, PQ 514-932-2582 Montreal Forum	

100

And so, at the age of thirty-one and having travelled all around the world, serving in one of the finest regiments on this earth and playing with such wonderful musicians, as 1987 came to an close, I started to think about what I would like to do in the future.

It was a gamble, what with having a mortgage and a wonderful wife and two children to look after, but in early January 1988, I had made, for me, a monumental decision. I woke up, sat up in bed and said to Mary, "I'm going into work this morning and am going to request my discharge by purchase." That is resign. With trepidation, I went to inform my Band Sergeant Major, Mick Dabbs, who with a tear in his eye, told me that I was destined to be a future BSM. Mick took me across the road to inform the Regimental Adjutant, Major Conway Seymour, who then took me in to see the Lt Col, Commanding the Regiment, Lt Col A Heroys. After a discussion in private, the three of them called me into an office and said that they would like to offer me three months leave to reconsider my decision.

On 30th March Major Seymour, the Regimental Adjutant telephoned me at home to ask if I had reconsidered my decision to leave. To which I replied "No Sir. I have had a wonderful time in the band, but it is now time to move on." The next day I went into Wellington Barracks, where the band had organised a wonderful farewell party and presentation for me. After 16 years and 225 days I left the army to pursue another career.

I feel that I must mention at this point, some of the wonderful musicians I worked with in the band, all highly skilled in their profession. The clarinet section had, for many years been the envy of other bands. When I first joined the band John Appleby was principal clarinet and then when he left the principal chair was shared between Tony Haigh (Aggie), Steve Hill and myself. However, those playing on 2nd and 3rd clarinet were equally skilled and competent to play on top stand. Aggie had the greatest influence on my playing. He had a brilliant technique and produced the sound that I wanted to emulate. Aggie also had a wicked sense of humour and was skilled in being able to make sounds or comments that I could hear sitting next to him that no one else could hear. On one occasion we were playing for the "Laying down of the Colours" in Ely Cathedral. The Queen was sitting only a few feet from us. The Ensign walked down the aisle of the Cathedral with the old Colour and then handed it over to a very elderly verger, who could hardly carry it. He then preceded to lift it on to the candle lit alter. Aggie then said, so that only I could hear him "Look, the silly old bugger is going to set light to it." Well, with the solemnity of the occasion, I just start corpsing as though my sides were going to split and I'm sure that Her Majesty picked up on this.

I now started out making a life for myself and my family as a freelancer and teacher and that exciting adventure is for another book.

This is not however, the end of the story as a Grenadier. As the motto goes, "Once a Grendier, always a Grenadier." My son, Chris, joined the band, as did my son- in- law Steve, both as clarinettists.

The Regimental Lieutenant Colonel is commanded by

The Colonel,
His Royal Highness The Prince Philip, Duke of Edinburgh
to invite you
to a Garden Party to mark the 350th Anniversary of the Grenadier Guards
at Buckingham Palace
on Monday 12th June 2006 from 3 to 6pm

in the presence of Her Majesty the Queen

Admission by personal security card only

On Monday 12th June 2006 Mary and myself, along with two dear friends were invited to a garden party at Buckingham Palace to Commemorate the 350th Anniversary of the Grenadier Guards. I, along with Steve and Chris had the honour of being presented to Her Majesty the Queen. The Queen was informed that I had served in the regimental band and that now my son and son- in- law were serving to which she replied "Well, one must keep it in the family musn't one."

Buckingham Palace, 12th June 2006

In writing this memoir, I have revisited so many exciting adventures and remembered so many dear friends. Some, I am still in contact with. Some, who are in my thoughts constantly, having passed away far, too young.

I am so thankful for the time I have spent with my family who proudly bear the name, The Band of the Grenadier Guards.

Printed in Great Britain
by Amazon

53724866R00066